Cambridge **Discovery Education**™

▶ **INTERACTIVE READERS**

Series editor: Bob Hastings

COOL JOBS

A1

David Maule

CAMBRIDGE
UNIVERSITY PRESS

Discovery
EDUCATION™

CAMBRIDGE UNIVERSITY PRESS
Cambridge, New York, Melbourne, Madrid, Cape Town,
Singapore, São Paulo, Delhi, Mexico City

Cambridge University Press
32 Avenue of the Americas, New York, NY 10013-2473, USA

www.cambridge.org
Information on this title: www.cambridge.org/9781107671607

First published 2014

Printed in Hong Kong, China, by Golden Cup Printing Company Limited

A catalog record for this publication is available from the British Library.

Library of Congress Cataloging-in-Publication Data

Maule, David.
 Cool jobs / David Maule.
    pages cm. -- (Cambridge discovery interactive readers)
  ISBN 978-1-107-67160-7 (pbk. : alk. paper)
  1. Work--Juvenile literature. 2. English language--Textbooks for foreign speakers. 3. Readers
(Elementary) I. Title.

HD4902.5.M38 2013
331.702--dc23

                              2013016880

ISBN 978-1-107-67160-7

Additional resources for this publication at www.cambridge.org

Cambridge University Press has no responsibility for the persistence or
accuracy of URLs for external or third-party Internet Web sites referred to in
this publication and does not guarantee that any content on such Web sites is,
or will remain, accurate or appropriate.

Layout services, art direction, book design, and photo research: Q2ABillSMITH GROUP
Editorial services: Hyphen S.A.
Audio production: CityVox, New York
Video production: Q2ABillSMITH GROUP

Distributed By:
Grass Roots Press
Toll Free: 1-888-303-3213
Fax: (780) 413-6582
Web Site: www.grassrootsbooks.net

Contents

Before You Read: Get Ready!

Some jobs can be in exciting places. Some jobs can work with fun machines. Do you know anyone with a really great job? Read on to learn about some cool jobs.

Words to Know

Complete the sentences with the correct words.

pilot   computer game designer   coal miner   nature photographer   sculptor

1 He has a hard job in a dark place. He's a

_____ .

2 Do you like computer games? Why not be a

_____ ?

3 She makes pieces of art called sculptures with her hands. She's a

_____ .

4 Do you like flying? Can you be a _____ ?

5 A _____ takes a lot of photos of plants and animals.

Words to Know

Complete the sentences with the correct words.

submarine

cruise ship

robot

1 My aunt makes food underwater. She is a cook on a
_____ .

2 It walks and talks, but it isn't a person. It's a
_____ .

3 My friend takes food to people on vacation on a boat. He's a waiter
on a _____ .

Some people travel for work.

CHAPTER 1

What's the Right Job for You?

MAYBE YOU HAVE A JOB OR MAYBE YOU ARE THINKING OF JOBS YOU CAN DO. HERE ARE SOME THINGS TO THINK ABOUT.

Head or Hands?

In some jobs you only think and speak and write. In other jobs you have to use your hands: you make things or make things work. In other jobs you design things on a computer.

Here or There?

Some people like to come home every night from work. Others enjoy traveling. They go to different countries and stay in hotels. But sometimes these people have to stay in difficult and **dangerous** places.

Working in the desert.

Working up high is dangerous.

Air, Sea, or Land?

Do you like flying in a plane? Do you like to be in or on water? Do you like big cities, small towns, or the country? Do you like hot places like deserts, or cold places like snowy mountains? People work in all kinds of places.

Safe or Dangerous?

Many people go to work every day and they come home – safe. That's true, but not for all people. Some jobs are dangerous. Some people do these jobs because they have to. There are no other jobs for them. Other people like doing dangerous jobs.

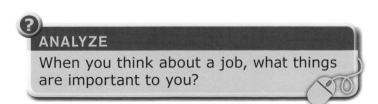

ANALYZE

When you think about a job, what things are important to you?

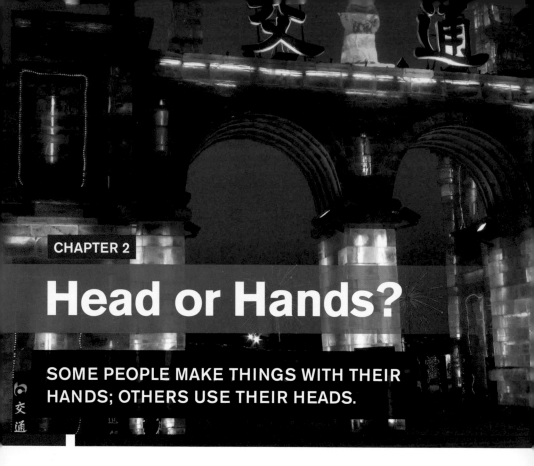

CHAPTER 2

Head or Hands?

SOME PEOPLE MAKE THINGS WITH THEIR HANDS; OTHERS USE THEIR HEADS.

Ice Sculptor

The city of Harbin is in China. In winter, it's very cold and people make things with ice and snow. Ma Yue comes from Harbin. He's a famous ice **sculptor**. But Ma Yue doesn't only work in Harbin. In 2010, people in Finland wanted to open an ice sculpture park, called Icium. Ma Yue took 60 ice sculptors there and they made a park. There are also ice parks in many other countries. In February, you can visit ice parks in Sapporo in Japan or in Quebec in Canada. In Quebec you can stay in an ice hotel. You can sleep on an ice bed, drink from an ice glass, and look out ice windows. It's all ice!

An ice hotel in Quebec

A roller coaster

Roller Coaster Designer

Do you like roller coasters? Some people do, some don't. Kent Seko really likes them. Roller coasters are his job – he designs them. In 1989 he helped to design a big roller coaster in Ohio, USA. This was the first roller coaster in the world to go up 60 meters. Now the highest roller coasters in the world go up 139 meters. Not all roller coaster **designers** want to ride on their roller coasters, but Kent does. He really enjoys it. When one of his new roller coasters opens, he's the first person on it. He loves it, and he doesn't have to pay!

Make-up

A funeral

Make-up for the Dead

Carrie Bayer is good with make-up, but she only works with dead[1] people. "Some years ago," she said, "I went to a funeral. I looked at the dead woman's make-up and I thought, 'I can do that better.' I was 33 years old, but I left my job. I went back to school and learned about make-up." And how does Carrie feel about the dead people? "I enjoy spending[2] time with them, and getting to know them in a way. Also, I think I help their families at a difficult time."

[1] **dead:** not living now
[2] **spend:** use time to do something or use money to buy something

Robot Maker

Amy Kukulya has a really great job. She works with underwater robots. She uses them to learn about the ocean.[3] She works with a robot that is very fast and can tell her a lot of things about the ocean.

An example of a robot that goes under the water

When Amy was a child, she loved playing in boats and catching fish. And now she's often on the water. She never thinks it's boring. Every day is different. Sometimes she makes parts for robots in Massachusetts. Other times she goes to Hawaii and works underwater. All the time she's learning and asking questions.

[3] **ocean:** the large bodies of salt water, like the Atlantic or Pacific

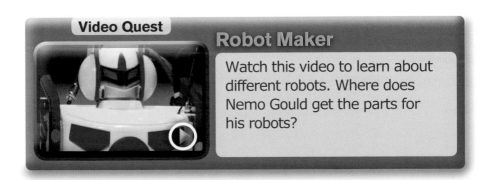

Video Quest

Robot Maker

Watch this video to learn about different robots. Where does Nemo Gould get the parts for his robots?

A game designer

CHAPTER 3

Playing Games

**DO YOU LIKE PLAYING COMPUTER GAMES?
WOULD YOU LIKE TO WORK WITH THEM?**

Ryan Shwayder is a game designer. It can be an interesting job, but it isn't all fun. He has to work many hours and he doesn't make a very good **salary**. He has to play many games, but he doesn't enjoy all of the games. Also, he has to think about the games. Why is this one good and this one not so good? And he has to read many books about games.

Another job with computer games is a game tester. Maybe you think it's a great job, but it's really not so easy. A game tester doesn't play a lot of different games every day. Game testers work on one game until it is ready for the factory. So they have to play again and again, and they have to find the problems. They have to talk to other game testers. Do you think it's a great job now?

Some people work with games from home. They are called **gold** farmers. In some computer games, players can make money. This isn't real money, it's game money. They can use it to buy things in the game. Gold farmers play a computer game for many hours to make a lot of game money. But they don't spend their game money

A game tester

to buy things in shops. It's gold to them because other players, all over the world, buy the game money from them – for US dollars! Then the other players spend it in the games they play.

?

EVALUATE

Why do people work as gold farmers?
Do you think they enjoy their job?

13

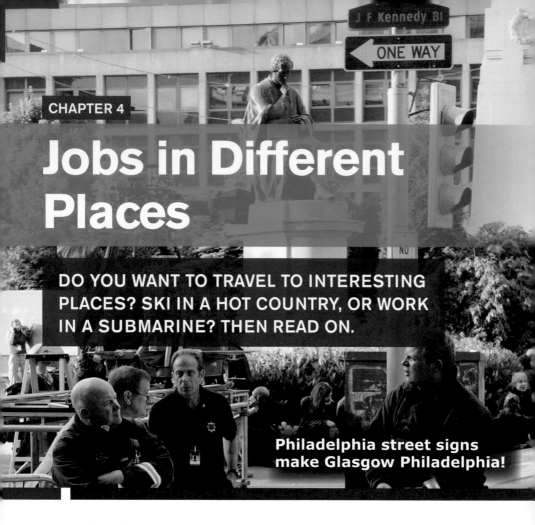

CHAPTER 4

Jobs in Different Places

DO YOU WANT TO TRAVEL TO INTERESTING PLACES? SKI IN A HOT COUNTRY, OR WORK IN A SUBMARINE? THEN READ ON.

Philadelphia street signs make Glasgow Philadelphia!

Location Scout

Look at the picture. This is from the movie, *World War* Z. This part of the movie is in Philadelphia – but this isn't Philadelphia. It's Glasgow, in Scotland. The movie makers came to Glasgow and changed it into an American city. They changed the Scottish street signs for American ones. But why did they do this? Why not make the movie in Philadelphia? Because sometimes it's cheaper or easier to make a film in another place.

Do you know this place? This is Hogwart's School in the Harry Potter films. Or is it? It's really Alnwick Castle in Northumberland, England. **Location scouts** travel all around the world to find good places for movies.

Cruise Ship Waitress

Gabriele Petrauskiené comes from Lithuania. Here she speaks about her job.

"I'm a waitress on a **cruise ship**. It's hard work – 70 hours a week. There are 1000 people on the ship and they eat a lot of food. I work six days and seven evenings a week. But I enjoy it because the ship goes to interesting places – the Caribbean, the Bahamas, Hawaii, and different parts of Europe. I visit nice places and see a lot of new things. On the ship we have parties, movies, and dance nights. Also, you can go to classes and learn lots of things, like new languages."

Cook on a submarine

Australia has three cooks on some of its submarines. They work together in a very small kitchen and make three big meals a day for up to 58 people. They have to travel a lot, and they can be away from home for six months. Food is very important for people on a submarine because life there can be really boring. It's not an easy job, but it pays well. The cooks make a salary up to 200,000 Australian dollars a year – that's about $205,000. The only person on the submarine to make a bigger salary is the captain![4]

[4] **captain:** the top person on a ship

People skiing

Snowmaker

Mark Simpson is a snowmaker. He works for Acer Snowmec in England. "We make places to ski inside," Mark says. "It really is snow – it looks like[5] snow and feels the same as snow in the Alps. And we can make many different kinds of snow." Mark goes to different countries, and sometimes he makes snow in the desert! "People from cold countries know about snow. But in a hot country, snow is something new. People don't know about it. It's interesting for the adults, but the children really love it."

[5]**looks like:** is almost the same as

Video Quest

Making Snow in the Desert

Watch this video to learn about making snow in the desert. What else can people do there?

CHAPTER 5

Dangerous Jobs

SOME PEOPLE HAVE DANGEROUS JOBS. YOU CAN READ ABOUT SOME OF THEM HERE.

Lewis Mitchell is a fisherman in Scotland. He says, "It's my father's boat. My brother also works on it. All the men in my family are fishermen." Fishing is a dangerous job. Many fishermen die every year, all over the world.

Carlos Jiménez is a coal miner in Colombia. Carlos says, "All my family live in this town. The job is dangerous. But there's no other work here, and I don't want to leave."

Carlos and Lewis have dangerous jobs. But there aren't many other jobs in their towns. But some people choose dangerous jobs. Let's look at one.

Simona Fraser is a pilot in Alaska. "I'm from Chicago," she says. "But I don't like big cities. So I studied at a college in Alaska. Then I learned to fly – a friend taught me. After college I went back to Chicago and got a job. But I wanted to live in Alaska. So I made some money and bought a small plane. Now people pay me, and I show them the animals. I love Alaska. It's very beautiful here."

But isn't flying dangerous? "Yes," she says. "But I don't worry too much."

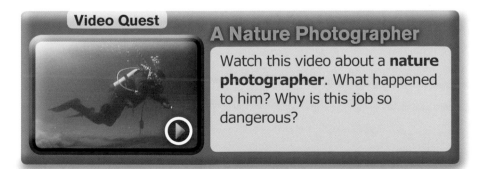

Video Quest

A Nature Photographer

Watch this video about a **nature photographer**. What happened to him? Why is this job so dangerous?

CHAPTER 6

What Do You Think?

WHICH PERSON IN THE BOOK IS ANSWERING THIS QUESTION?

"WHAT ARE THE GOOD AND BAD THINGS ABOUT YOUR JOB?"

"I VISIT A LOT OF INTERESTING PLACES, BUT I HAVE TO WORK 70 HOURS A WEEK."

Now think about these jobs. Think about one good thing and one bad thing for each job.

- ice sculptor
- game designer
- location scout
- submarine cook
- pilot
- nature photographer

Think of the things you like. Look at these:

I like …

- ❑ water
- ❑ computers
- ❑ to cook
- ❑ to travel and see new places

- ❑ movies
- ❑ ice and snow
- ❑ to work inside
- ❑ places with no people

- ❑ animals
- ❑ flying
- ❑ to work with my hands
- ❑ dangerous things

Now think about three fun jobs for you. What are they? Why are they good for you?

"I want to be a nature photographer because I like animals, and I want to travel and see new places."

After You Read

Which jobs are these? Read again what people from this book say about their jobs. Then match the names of the jobs from the box with the sentences below.

> a. submarine cook   b. cruise ship waitress   c. fisherman
> d. gold farmer   e. ice sculptor   f. location scout   g. pilot
> h. robot maker   i. roller coaster designer   j. snowmaker

1 I make cold places in hot countries. _____

2 I help people to learn about the ocean with machines that I make. _____

3 I work many hours a week, but I see interesting places and learn new things. _____

4 I travel to different countries and find places to make movies. _____

5 I make things, but they only stay for a short time, then I have to make new ones. _____

6 My job is dangerous, but I love it here because it's beautiful. _____

7 They pay me a lot of money because not many people want to do my job. _____

8 I work from home and make money with my computer. _____

9 I make things and I'm always the first to ride on them. _____

10 My father and my brother do the same dangerous job. _____

True or False

Read the sentences and choose Ⓐ (True) or Ⓑ (False).
If the book does not tell you, choose Ⓒ (Doesn't say).

1 Carrie Bayer learned to do a new job at the age of 33.

Ⓐ True
Ⓑ False
Ⓒ Doesn't say

2 Ryan Shwayder started to design computer games at school.

Ⓐ True
Ⓑ False
Ⓒ Doesn't say

3 Gold farmers don't go out and look for gold.

Ⓐ True
Ⓑ False
Ⓒ Doesn't say

4 Life is always interesting on a submarine.

Ⓐ True
Ⓑ False
Ⓒ Doesn't say

5 Mark Simpson made snow in Dubai.

Ⓐ True
Ⓑ False
Ⓒ Doesn't say

6 Lewis Mitchell's father is a fisherman.

Ⓐ True
Ⓑ False
Ⓒ Doesn't say

Answer Key

Words to Know, page 4

1 coal miner **2** computer game designer **3** sculptor
4 pilot **5** nature photographer

Words to Know, page 5

1 submarine **2** robot **3** cruise ship

Analyze, page 7
Answers will vary.

Video Quest, page 11
He finds old things and uses them.

Evaluate, page 13
Answers will vary.

Video Quest, page 17
Answers will vary.

Video Quest, page 19
He got very cold and had to be warmed up. It's very cold
under the ice.

Match, page 22
1 j **2** h **3** b **4** f **5** e **6** g **7** a **8** d **9** i **10** c

True or False, page 23
1 A **2** C **3** A **4** B **5** C **6** A